MW00460644

A 30-Day Evangelism Plan

Len Andyshak

Developing the Habit of Loving People

INTERVARSITY PRESS
DOWNERS GROVE, ILLINOIS 60515

Second edition © 1986 by Inter-Varsity Christian Fellowship of the United States of America.

© 1982 by Inter-Varsity Christian Fellowship of the United States of America.

InterVarsity Press is the book-publishing division of Inter-Varsity Christian Fellowship, a student movement active on campus at hundreds of universities, colleges and schools of nursing. For information about local and regional activities, write IVCF, 6400 Schroeder Rd., P.O. Box 7895, Madison, WI 53707-7895.

Worksheets 2 and 3 are from Tell the Truth *by Will Metzger (IVP).*

Distributed in Canada through InterVarsity Press, 860 Denison St., Unit 3, Markham, Ontario L3R 4H1, Canada.

ISBN 0-87784-218-3

Printed in the United States of America

13	12	11	10	9	8	7	6	5	4	3	2
96	95	94	93	92	91	90	89	88			

Once upon a time there was a young, itinerant Jewish preacher. He was outspoken, to say the least. He often said many strange things. He once said, "Follow me, and I will make you fishers of men." Later he said, "Go fish in all nations," or something pretty close to that. Ever since then, those of us who have become disciples of this person have realized that we are to become fishers of men and to go to all the world, telling people about this preacher, Jesus Christ.

We often feel, however, that our attempts at fishing are inadequate . . . or we simply do no fishing at all. It has been said that a person learns fishing only by fishing. But how do you get started? How do you keep going? There are many possible ways. This pamphlet presents one. It is meant to be simple and practical—simple enough to be used by anyone and practical enough to do the job. It does not depend on our background or skills. But it does depend on the Lord, since the whole endeavor is absolutely miraculous.

What's involved?

There are seven basic activities suggested over a 30–day period.

1. Daily prayer
2. Daily reading
3. Meeting people
4. Spending casual time with people
5. Inviting friends
6. Asking about Jesus
7. Choosing a next step

The focus in these seven activities is not be on techniques or on honing secret skills guaranteed to usher even the most skeptical atheist into the kingdom. Rather our time over these thirty days will be spent developing the habit of loving people and being a friendly Christian. Let me share a few reasons for aiming in this direction.

First, love is the essence of what Jesus has called us to! The two great commandments are to love God and to love our neighbors. We have not been called primarily to a task, but to a relationship and to a transformed character. Sharing the good news is not merely a religious activity but the overflow of our love for both the Lord and those around us. Christians must be known as lovers and servants, not salespeople. Too often Christians talk a lot *about* Jesus but have little of his deep and practical love for people.

Second, love is not dependent on which gifts or experiences we possess. Neither is love an involuntary emotion that wells up inside us. It is an action of care and concern for others. The Lord increasingly enables us to choose to love those around us. As we give our lives away to others, the Lord accomplishes his purposes in surprising ways.

Finally, this 30-day plan is meant to be a beginning, not an ending. As we do more fishing, we will collect equipment and skills and information. For now the important matter is to begin at the beginning.

This 30-day evangelism plan can be done alone, but I would suggest doing it with one or more friends. That way you can encourage each other to be accountable to one another. While the plan is simple, I have found that many people start with good intentions and much enthusiasm only to falter along the way. You and your friends may therefore want to add an eighth activity—spending time together each week to share and pray about the other seven activities.

Before you start you might want to review the basics of the gospel. Worksheet 1 on page 25 is a helpful summary that you may want to be familiar with. You could even practice sharing and discussing these gospel basics with a friend just to build your confidence a bit. Worksheet 3 (pp. 28-31) gives some possible role plays to use.

Now let's outline the details.

1. Daily Prayer
For 30 days begin each day with a simple,

specific prayer; an example would be something like this: "Here I am, Lord; please heal me, strengthen me, introduce me to the people you want me to love, and please give me opportunities to share with them about you. Amen."

Check this off each day on the weekly progress charts included at the end of this pamphlet.

One of the key phrases which came from the Urbana 84 missions convention was the statement from Eric Alexander that "prayer is not preparation for the battle; prayer is the battle." Many people have shared with me during and after this 30-day experience that they were amazed at what the Lord had done once they simply started praying daily about their outreach. If you develop only the habit of daily prayer as a result of your 30 days, the program will certainly have been worth it.

2. Daily Reading
During the 30 days you will also be reading a book—five pages a day. Reading just these few pages each day provides continued training and encouragement with-

out becoming a burden. This could easily fit into your daily devotional time.

Three good options are Rebecca Pippert's *Out of the Saltshaker,* Tom Eisenman's *Everyday Evangelism* or Will Metzger's *Tell the Truth,* all from IVP. Check off this reading on your chart each day to keep you going.

3. Meeting People

Over the 30 days your goal will be to introduce yourself to fifteen to twenty new people. This can be done anyway or anywhere you desire. To put it another way, you can meet people anyway the Lord leads as he answers your prayers for daily opportunities. Perhaps it will be sitting by someone in class, saying hello and exchanging names. It could be while you are shopping in a store, running, riding a bus or going up in a hot-air balloon . . . who knows what the Lord may do?

Rather than merely checking this on your chart, you'll find it very helpful to record the names of those you meet. If you review these daily it will help you to pray for them and be able to call them by name when you see them next. This is a practical way to express love, and you'll find people appreciative that you actually remembered their names.

I'll never forget one shy woman who told me that after only one week she had already met thirteen people! I was amazed. She had realized that there was no pressure for her to perform. She saw how the Lord virtually introduced her to one person after another.

Obviously, to share the gospel with people we must meet them and be with them first. And certainly people were a priority for Jesus. He was always out in the streets with people. His life was an adventure of rubbing shoulders with an amazing variety of folk. None of us has the relational skills of Jesus, but the Lord is anxious to use even the small risks we take to do his work.

4. Casual Times

Four times during the month (roughly once a week) spend some time with a non-Christian friend or acquaintance. It could be the same person each time or four different people. Possibly it will be one of the fifteen to twenty new people you've met. This is to be a casual, nonreligious activity of some kind. Go have a Coke, drop in at their place to visit, go to a ball game or a party, study together, go jog or whatever. Just be with them and enjoy their company. Sounds strangely like being a friend, doesn't it?

Record the when, where and what of these activities on your chart.

While we see Jesus meeting people in the Gospels, we also see him enjoying and befriending them. The Pharisees were frustrated because he went to the tax collectors' parties and even his own disciples were upset with him because he wouldn't send the crowds away. Jesus did not simply love people in some metaphysical way. He made them a central part of his life. Time with them was not a project or an occasional event. We must also learn the joy of focusing our lives on those who need us.

5. Invitations
Four other times (once a week again), in–

vite one of your non-Christian friends to a "religious" activity of some type that you feel is appropriate. They don't have to accept; you just have to invite them! The invitation could be to church, to a Bible study, to a movie, to a fellowship meeting, to an evangelistic talk or potluck. You could even be daring and invite them to look at Jesus in the Bible with you for a few weeks.

As you might have guessed, there is a place on your chart for this.

I always think about Levi throwing a party for all of his tax-collector buddies to meet Jesus (Lk 5:27-32). You get the impression that a lot of them came. One of the nice things about invitations like this is that you aren't asking a person to make the final leap to conversion. It just gives them a chance to take a step closer in the safety of your friendship.

6. Asking about Jesus

Twice during this month-long adventure, your task is to simply ask a person what they think about Jesus. You might start by first asking about their church background and if they're still involved. Then move to the question of Jesus. These couple of questions will get you to the heart of the matter easily and quickly. Then it's just a matter of having a short conversation about Jesus just as you would about a class, a news event or your families. Ask a few more questions that their comments raise in your mind. For example, "Why did you stop going to church?" or, "How did you come to your conclusions about Jesus?" Then feel free to share some of your responses. You'll find people surprisingly open with you, especially after having established even a brief friendship with you before this point.

As always, the key is to be sensitive to the Lord's guidance—the right person (perhaps not the one you expected) at the right time (perhaps at an inconvenient moment or when you are sure you're not yet ready). Often an opportunity will open up when you are inviting your friend to an activity.

Remember that simple prayer you pray each day? God will indeed hear, and he will indeed answer. You can *expect* God to provide some miraculous opportunities and the wisdom from above in that moment. " 'Not by might, nor by power, but by my Spirit,' says the Lord" (Zech 4:6).

7. Taking the Next Step

At the end of this 30 days of adventure you are through beginning, but hopefully anything but ready to stop. Now it will be time to choose one or two or three specific goals to continue your momentum in the immediate future. The goal is to continue fostering a lifestyle like that of Jesus who was always out there loving people in the street.

Let me list a few of the many possibilities to get your imagination moving. Choose something that excites you and seems to fit you at this point.

☐ Pray daily for non–Christian friends.

☐ Eat a meal with someone new twice a week.

☐ Volunteer to tutor a student who is weak in a subject you know well.

☐ Join an evangelistic drama or music group.

☐ Do the 30-day plan again—or adopt parts of it as regular practice.

☐ Join a club to increase your involve-
ment with non-Christians.

☐ Join a prison ministry.

☐ Start an investigative Bible study for
your non-Christian friends.

☐ Adopt an elderly person to visit reg-
ularly.

☐ Befriend a young child who is lonely.

☐ Memorize an outline of the gospel.

☐ Study a part of the gospel in depth.

☐ Study answers to questions most
asked by seekers.

There is a page to help you formulate the
specifics of your plan at the end of this
pamphlet.

Well, that's about it. I hope the prospect
of spending the next 30 days loving people
excites you more than scares you. I think
Jesus purposely arranged things so that it
always takes some faith to follow him. The
wonderful thing is that following him always leads to richer and fuller living. Can
it be that his commands to love and fish
are part of his plan to make us whole as
well as those to whom we go?

Have a miraculous 30 days of walking
beside the Jesus of the Gospels and watch-

ing him transform you and all of those people he takes you to meet!

Before You Start

1. Consider doing this with some friends.
Write their names here if you agree to
meet them weekly.

2. Go through Worksheets 1 and 2 (pp. 25–
26) with a friend.

Week One

	Date	Prayer	Reading (book/page numbers)
Day 1	___	___	_____
Day 2	___	___	_____
Day 3	___	___	_____
Day 4	___	___	_____
Day 5	___	___	_____
Day 6	___	___	_____
Day 7	___	___	_____

_____

This week I met . . .

I had casual times with . . .

I gave invitations to . . .

I discussed Jesus with . . .

Week Two

	Date	Prayer	Reading (book/page numbers)
Day 8	____	____	_____
Day 9	____	____	_____
Day 10	____	____	_____
Day 11	____	____	_____
Day 12	____	____	_____
Day 13	____	____	_____
Day 14	____	____	_____

_____

This week I met . . .

I had casual times with . . .

I gave invitations to . . .

I discussed Jesus with . . .

Week Three

	Date	Prayer	Reading (book/page numbers)
Day 15	____	____	_____
Day 16	____	____	_____
Day 17	____	____	_____
Day 18	____	____	_____
Day 19	____	____	_____
Day 20	____	____	_____
Day 21	____	____	_____

_____

This week I met . . .

I had casual times with . . .

I gave invitations to . . .

I discussed Jesus with . . .

Week Four

	Date	Prayer	Reading (book/page numbers)
Day 22	_____	_____	_____
Day 23	_____	_____	_____
Day 24	_____	_____	_____
Day 25	_____	_____	_____
Day 26	_____	_____	_____
Day 27	_____	_____	_____
Day 28	_____	_____	_____
Day 29	_____	_____	_____

This week I met . . .

I had casual times with . . .

I gave invitations to . . .

I discussed Jesus with . . .

Day 30

My Next Step

Goals:

1.

2.

3.

Needed:

First step:

Date starting:

Now that you've finished, I'd like to share one more word about the results you have, or haven't, seen. Ultimately, as Jesus told us (Jn 12:32), he is the one who draws people to himself. Our part is to be faithful witnesses. If we are doing this, we are a success, and the Lord is always pleased with our obedience (2 Cor 2:15–16).

You may have found yourself in an office or on a dorm floor or in a neighborhood where the people around you simply are not responding to the Lord's call through you. If this is so, what do you do? The answer is that you are to love them for another 30 days and then another and then . . . Remember that we don't merely love people who are responsive or even just so that they will respond. We love them because to love is the wonderful assignment we have been given by the God who reaches out to the world that resists him.

At the same time, however, throw your nets over the other side of the boat. There are other opportunities for witness. Don't abandon the relationships God has given you. Just keep praying, fishing and expecting surprising things to happen.

Worksheet 1

First Steps to God ——————————————

Here is an outline that summarizes the main points of the gospel in four words: *God, Man, Christ, Response*. To be faithful to the gospel, we must convey the vital truth clustering around each of these words.

God ——————————————————————

God loves you (Jn 3:16).

God is holy and just. He punishes all evil and expels it from his presence (Rom 1:18).

Man ——————————————————————

God, who created everything, made us for himself to find our purpose in fellowship with him (Col 1:16).

But we rebelled and turned away from God (Is 53:6). The result is separation from God (Is 59:2). The penalty is eternal death (Rom 6:23).

Christ ——————————————————————

God became a human being in the person of Jesus Christ to restore the broken fellowship (Col 1:19–20a). Christ lived a perfect life (1 Pet 2:22).

Christ died as a substitute for us by paying the death penalty for our rebellion (Rom 5:8). He arose and is alive today to give us a new life of fellowship with God, now and forever (1 Cor 15:3–4; Jn 10:10).

Response ——————————————————

I must *repent* for my rebellion (Mt 4:17).

I must *believe* Christ died to provide forgiveness and a new life of fellowship with God (Jn 1:12).

I must *receive* Christ as my Savior and Lord with the intent to obey him. I do this in prayer by inviting him into my life (Rev 3:20).

Worksheet 2

Personal Testimony _____

This is *your* spiritual autobiography. Many Christians are unable to point to a crisis experience, or we do not always know the date when God brought us into his kingdom (perhaps he did so when we were young). This does not mean you have nothing to testify about. Be winsome, honest and wholesome. Never go into detail about sins. After a person has heard your story, will they know basic truths about Christ, or only know you better? Use *some* of the phrases under each heading to help you focus on important things.

1. What I Was Like _____

My family, friends, interests were . . .

My security (most important value) was . . .

My religious background and attitude about Christ was . . .

2. What God Used to Begin to Open My Eyes_

I was awakened to my need by (people, books, meeting, circumstances) . . .

What I thought and/or noticed (about myself, God, others) at this point was . . .

3. What It Was I Saw/Understood _____
Those aspects of the gospel that touched me were . . .

I came to understand that Christ . . .

I saw my need was . . .

4. How Christ Has/Is Affecting My Life_____
My relationships with . . .

My attitude toward . . .

My desires now are . . .

I'm now doing . . .

A difficult area of obedience is . . .

Worksheet 3

Four Role Plays _____
A. Gospel Overview Presentation _____

Setting: Think of a non–Christian friend with whom you have had some opportunity to share certain aspects of Christian truth. This friend, by his or her reactions (confusion, criticism, questions) obviously doesn't understand what you're talking about.

Procedure: First person assumes role of a Christian and begins with a statement similar to this: "You know, we've talked about Christianity a couple of times but I get the impression that I'm not communicating what I really mean. Can I give you an overview of where I'm coming from? Perhaps by giving you a frame of reference for some of my statements we can communicate better. How about hearing me out—saving your questions till the end?"

Second person assumes role of a semi-interested non–Christian. He or she remains attentive for the presentation, not asking any questions, and concludes by saying, "Interesting. Let me think about this and then we'll talk some more." This person then gives feedback to the Christian on how well they did/didn't do in expressing themselves.

Time: Overview of entire gospel—20 minutes. Bible can be used but not notes. Evaluation of presentation—10 minutes. Evaluate content, illustrations, body language.

Other Ideas: You can switch roles and let the second person try if you add another half-hour. You can take a full hour with the second person asking questions for clarification (not raising objections) instead of remaining silent during the overview.

B. Answering Questions of Non-Christians_____
Setting: There are about a dozen recurring questions which non-Christians ask about the gospel. By beginning to get a handle on how to answer these, you can both help people and steer the conversation back to the real question, "What will you do with Christ?" While realizing that often these questions are a smokescreen hiding their real self and needs, nevertheless there are times when they are asked honestly. Pick one of the following questions:

1. Is the Bible trustworthy?
2. Is Christ the only way to God?
3. Why does a good God allow suffering and evil?
4. Isn't one person's opinion as good as another's, since no one can really know what is true?
5. I try to do my best, so won't my good efforts get me to heaven?

Procedure: First person assumes role of non-Christian asking one of the questions. Ask additional questions to clarify as needed. Second person tries to answer them.

Time: Dialog—15-minute minimum. Evaluation of answers—5 minutes.

Other Ideas: Switch roles for the next 20 minutes. This exercise could also be done in small groups, that is with a number of others observing the dialog between two people.

C. Voicing the Objections of Your Non-Christian Friends _____
Setting: Think of a non-Christian friend or relative that you know well enough to know their objections to Christian beliefs.

Procedure: First person assumes role of their non-

Christian friend, consistently reacting the way the friend would in the ensuing dialog with a Christian. First person begins by saying, "Well, my problem with Christianity is . . ."Second person plays a Christian. The task is to listen and draw out the non-Christian and seek to answer.

Time: Dialog—15-minute minimum. Evaluation of each other—10 minutes.

Other Ideas: Switch roles for the next 25 minutes. This is a good situation to include a third person who merely observes what the first two are saying and gives feedback to both.

D. Finding Out Someone's Level of Interest ___

Setting: Your non-Christian friend has been thinking about some of your talks together. He or she has actually started to become interested! But you don't know how much. How can you find out?

Procedure: First person plays role of one of their interested non-Christian friends. They pick *one* of three possible levels of interest without telling the other person what level is chosen: (1) intrigued enough to read a booklet; (2) interested enough to come to a Bible study; (3) wants to find out how to become a Christian. Maintain that level throughout the dialog. All questions and all statements should be made according to the appropriate level of interest. The goal of the second person is to find out how interested the other one is without immediately asking, for example, "Would you like to come to a Bible study?"

Time: Dialog—15 minutes.

Other Ideas: Switch roles. Pray then and there for your non-Christian friends.

Suggestions for Further Reading

Rebecca M. Pippert, *Out of the Saltshaker* (IVP). A basic guide to evangelism as a natural way of life. paper, 192 pages

Will Metzger, *Tell the Truth* (IVP). A comprehensive presentation of what it means for whole people to offer the whole gospel to the whole person; includes many practical suggestions. paper, 141 pages

Tom Eisenman, *Everyday Evangelism* (IVP). The best way to attract people to the gospel is with the sweet aroma of God's love. Here's a motivating look at how to do just that. paper, 192 pages (available Spring 1987)

Don Posterski, *Why Am I Afraid to Tell You I'm a Christian?* (IVP). He shows how to win people to Christ by using Jesus' own approach—caring deeply and presenting the gospel in a way that matters. paper, 96 pages

Paul Little, *How to Give Away Your Faith* (IVP). Practical advice for realistic communication of the gospel. paper, 131 pages

John R. W. Stott, *Basic Christianity* (IVP). A clear presentation of the fundamental content of Christianity. paper, 142 pages

Cliffe Knechtle, *Give Me an Answer* (IVP). Answers forty of the most-often asked questions by non-Christians. paper, 156 pages